Creating the PEACEABLE SCHOOL

Creating the PEACEABLE SCHOOL

A Comprehensive Program for Teaching Conflict Resolution

Student Manual

Richard J. Bodine ✦ Donna K. Crawford ✦ Fred Schrumpf

Research Press   2612 North Mattis Avenue   Champaign, Illinois 61821

The illustration on page 11 has been reprinted with the kind permission
of Quaker Peace and Service, London, England.

The first two definitions of peace on page 42 are quoted from, respectively, "Gifts, Not Stars" (p. 553)
by George E. Lyon, in *Horn Book, September-October,* 1992; and *Peace Begins With You* (p. 33)
by Katherine Scholes, 1990, San Franciso: Little, Brown.

The principles of conflict resolution on page 50 are derived from *Getting to Yes* (2nd ed.)
by Roger Fisher, William Ury, and Bruce Patton, 1991, New York: Penguin.

Adaptations of the classic Red Riding Hood story appearing on page 82 and thereafter
are based on a retelling in *Individual Development: Creativity* by Leif Fearn, 1974, San
Diego: Education Improvement Associates.

Copies of this book may be ordered from the publisher at the address given on the title page.

Cover design by Linda Brown
Composition by Tradewinds Imaging
Printed by Malloy Lithographing

ISBN 0-87822-350-9
Library of Congress Catalog Number 94-67021

Contents

SECTION 3   **Understanding Peace and Peacemaking**

SECTION 4   **Mediation**

SECTION 1

Building a Peaceable Climate

Introduction

IMAGINE . . .

- ♦ A school where you and your peers peacefully resolve your conflicts

- ♦ A classroom where you work together with peers . . . trusting, helping, and sharing

- ♦ A lunchroom where you observe carefully, communicate accurately, and listen to understand

- ♦ A playground where you respect, appreciate, and celebrate your differences

- ♦ A principal's office where you express feelings, particularly anger and frustration, in ways that do not hurt others

This is the vision of the peaceable school. In the peaceable school, all of these behaviors happen in each of these places.

WHAT YOU WILL LEARN

To help you build a peaceable school, you will learn about:

- ◆ The class meeting

- ◆ Rights and responsibilities

- ◆ Rules

- ◆ Cooperation

To help you understand how to get along, you will learn about:

- ◆ Conflict

- ◆ Peace and peacemaking

To help you resolve problems, you will learn about:

- ◆ Negotiation

- ◆ Mediation

- ◆ Group problem solving

Ground Rules for the Class Meeting

RULE 1   Participants sit in a circle.

RULE 2   Every member of the class is responsible for communication (*listening and speaking*).

RULE 3   The *"Rule of Focus"* applies to all discussion. This means that whoever is speaking will be allowed to talk without being interrupted.

RULE 4   Participants show respect for others. This means no criticism or sarcasm toward group members or their ideas.

RULE 5   Each time someone in the group finishes making a statement, another group member summarizes and clarifies it before anyone else goes on to a new idea.

The class meeting is a strategy that will help build a peaceable school.

What Responsibility Means to Me

INSTRUCTIONS: In the boxes write words or draw pictures that come to mind when you think of responsibility.

RESPONSIBILITY

Peace is a responsibility.

What Rights Mean to Me

INSTRUCTIONS: Write or draw some things you think students have the right to do.

RIGHTS

Peace is a right.

Rights and Responsibilities

RESPONSIBILITIES ARE . . .

- ◆ Something you are always expected to do

- ◆ A way you are always expected to act

- ◆ A way you are expected to treat someone else

RIGHTS ARE . . .

- ◆ Guaranteed conditions
  (what you should always expect)

Enjoying a right requires everyone to
accept certain responsibilities.

My Rights and Responsibilities

INSTRUCTIONS: Write some of your own rights and responsibilities.

RIGHTS

Example: I have the right to be myself and be respected.

_____

_____

_____

_____

_____

_____

_____

_____

_____

RESPONSIBILITIES

Example: I have the responsibility to respect others, even if they are different from me.

_____

_____

_____

_____

_____

_____

_____

_____

_____

Rules for Our Class

INSTRUCTIONS: Write five rules for our class.

RULE 1 _____

_____

_____

RULE 2 _____

_____

_____

RULE 3 _____

_____

_____

RULE 4 _____

_____

_____

RULE 5 _____

_____

_____

Rules let everyone know his or her responsibilities
and safeguard the rights of all.

Cooperation

Understanding Conflict

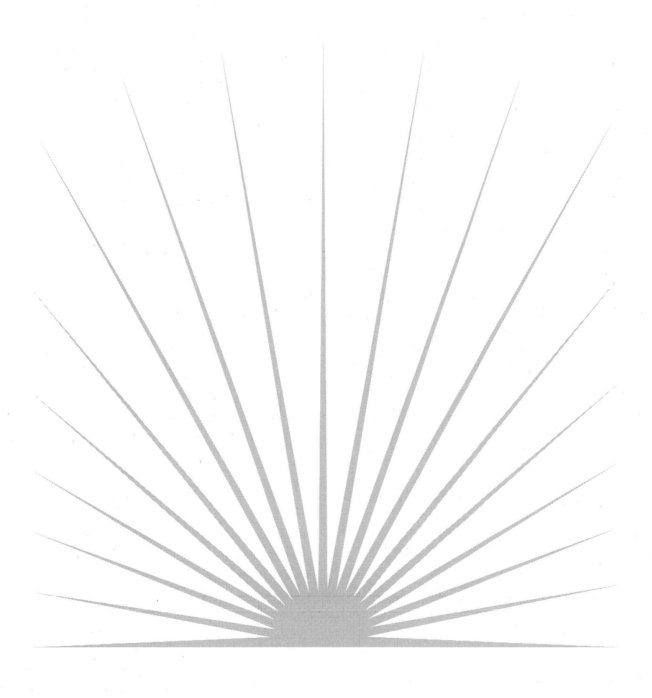

What Conflict Means to Me

INSTRUCTIONS: In the boxes write words or draw pictures that come to mind when you think of conflict.

CONFLICT

Ideas About Conflict

♦ Conflicts are a natural part of everyday life.

♦ Conflicts can be handled in positive or negative ways.

♦ Conflicts are an opportunity to learn and grow.

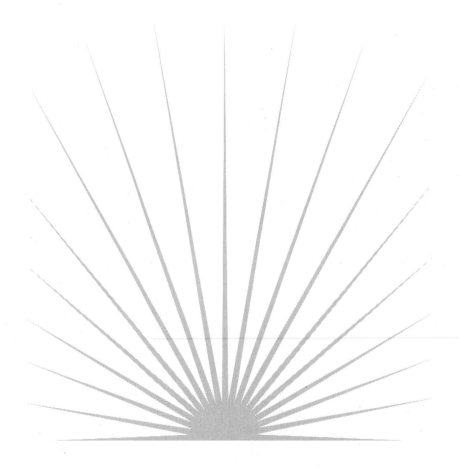

Basic Needs

BELONGING

POWER

FREEDOM

FUN

Understanding how to resolve a conflict begins with identifying the origin of the conflict. Most every conflict between people involves the attempt to meet basic needs for belonging, power, freedom, or fun.

How We Meet Our Basic Needs

♦ Our **BELONGING** need is met by developing relationships with others where we have the opportunity to love, share, and cooperate.

♦ Our **POWER** need is met by achieving, accomplishing, and being recognized and respected.

♦ Our **FREEDOM** need is met by making choices in our lives.

♦ Our **FUN** need is met by laughing and playing.

We are all born with the same basic needs. However, the things we each choose to do to meet these needs may be different from what others choose.

How I Meet My Basic Needs

INSTRUCTIONS: In each need shape, draw or write some things you do to meet your basic needs.

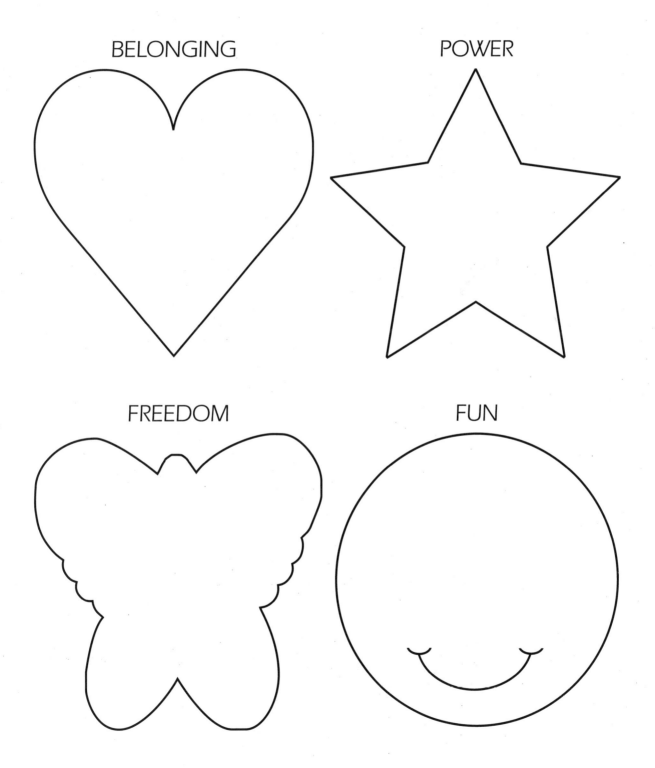

BELONGING

POWER

FREEDOM

FUN

Looking at My Conflicts

INSTRUCTIONS: In each need shape, draw or write some examples of conflicts you have experienced.

BELONGING

POWER

FREEDOM

FUN

Enough Is Not Enough

INSTRUCTIONS: Draw two conflicts you have experienced that involved limited resources. Next make lines from these drawings to the shapes to show what basic needs also caused these conflicts.

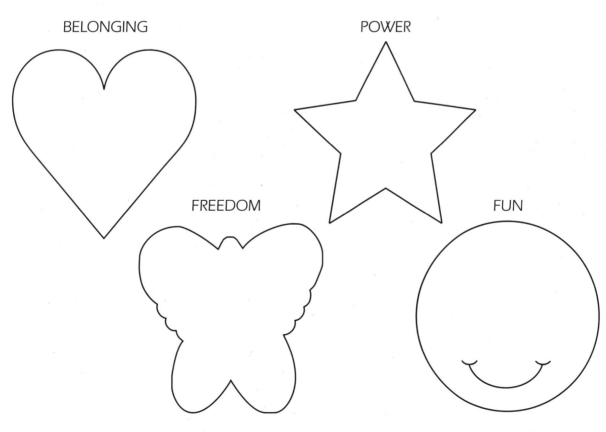

BELONGING

POWER

FREEDOM

FUN

Different Values

INSTRUCTIONS: Draw two conflicts you have experienced that involved different values. Next make lines from these drawings to the shapes to show what basic needs also caused these conflicts.

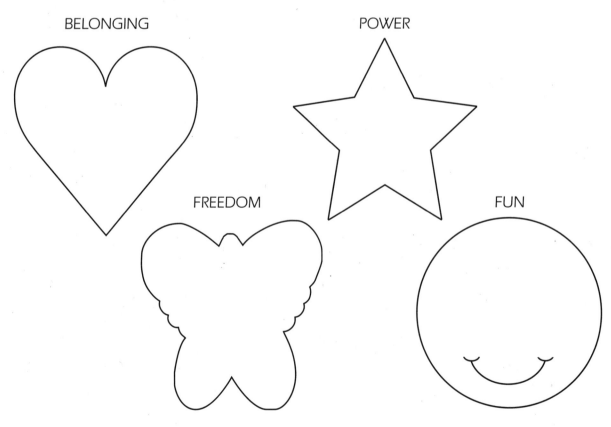

BELONGING

POWER

FREEDOM

FUN

Origins of Conflict

LIMITED RESOURCES	UNMET BASIC NEEDS	DIFFERENT VALUES
Time	Belonging	Beliefs
Money	Power	Priorities
Property	Freedom	Principles
	Fun	

CONFLICT

Limited resources and different values
can be the causes of conflict. Unmet needs
are also a part of conflicts over limited
resources and different values.

Origins of My Conflicts

INSTRUCTIONS: In each need shape, draw or write examples of conflicts you have experienced where you did not get your basic needs met.

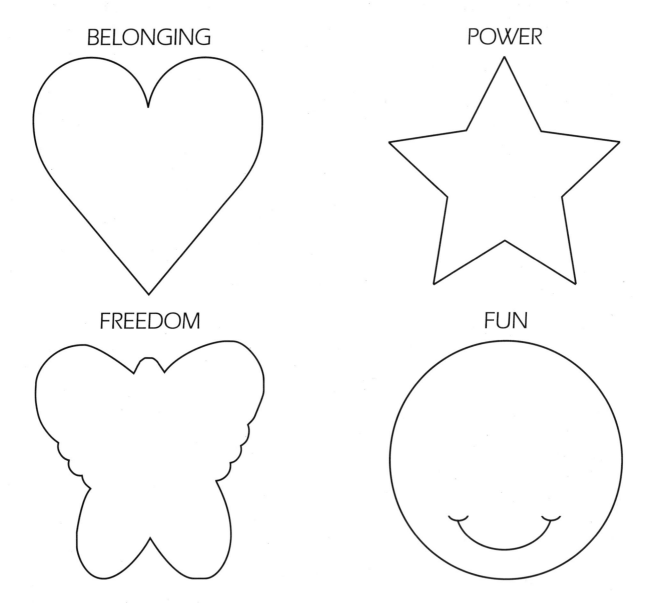

BELONGING

POWER

FREEDOM

FUN

♦ Were any of these conflicts also caused by limited resources (time, money, property)?

♦ Were any of these conflicts also caused by different values (beliefs, priorities, principles)?

How I Respond to Conflict

INSTRUCTIONS: Put a check mark in the boxes that show the responses that are most typical for you when you are in conflict with another person. Then circle the three responses you normally make first in a conflict.

	OFTEN	SOMETIMES	NEVER
Yell back or threaten the person	☐	☐	☐
Avoid or ignore the person	☐	☐	☐
Change the subject	☐	☐	☐
Try to understand the other side	☐	☐	☐
Complain to an adult	☐	☐	☐
Call the other person names	☐	☐	☐
Let the person have his or her way	☐	☐	☐
Try to reach a compromise	☐	☐	☐
Let an adult decide who is right	☐	☐	☐
Talk to find ways to agree	☐	☐	☐
Apologize	☐	☐	☐
Hit or push back	☐	☐	☐
Cry	☐	☐	☐
Make it into a joke	☐	☐	☐
Pretend my feelings are not hurt	☐	☐	☐

Soft Responses to Conflict

Sometimes we have a soft response to conflict. Have you ever:

♦ Ignored a conflict, hoping it would go away?

♦ Denied that a conflict mattered?

♦ Withdrawn from a situation and not shared what you were feeling?

♦ Given in just to be nice?

INSTRUCTIONS: Write or draw an example of a conflict in which you responded in a soft way.

SOFT

Hard Responses to Conflict

Sometimes we have a hard response to conflict. Have you ever:

- ◆ Threatened?

- ◆ Pushed?

- ◆ Hit?

- ◆ Yelled?

INSTRUCTIONS: Write or draw an example of a conflict in which you responded in a hard way.

HARD

Principled Responses to Conflict

A third type of response to conflict is a principled response. Have you ever:

- ◆ Listened with the intent to understand the other person's point of view?

- ◆ Showed respect for differences?

- ◆ Looked for ways to resolve the problem that will help everyone involved?

PRINCIPLED

Responses to Conflict

SOFT RESPONSE	HARD RESPONSE	PRINCIPLED RESPONSE
Withdrawing	Threatening	Listening
Ignoring	Pushing	Understanding
Denying	Hitting	Respecting
Giving in	Yelling	Resolving

INSTRUCTIONS: Answer the questions below for each possible response to conflict.

RESPONSES	Are basic needs getting met?	How do people feel?	Will things get better or worse?
Soft			
Hard			
Principled			

Outcomes of Conflict

LOSE-LOSE

WIN-LOSE

WIN-WIN

Conflicts result in winning or losing outcomes
depending on the responses we choose.

Five Scenes

SCENE 1

Tanya: *(Tosses balloon in the air, having fun by herself.)*

Eric: I want to play with you. *(Tries to join Tanya by tapping balloon up in the air.)*

Tanya: *(Calmly)* I had it first. *(Ignores Eric and continues to hit the balloon.)*

Eric: *(Watches Tanya, looks sad, and walks away.)*

SCENE 2

Tanya: *(Tosses balloon in the air, having fun by herself.)*

Eric: I want to play with you. *(Tries to join Tanya by tapping balloon up in the air.)*

Tanya: *(Calmly)* I had it first.

Eric: *(Calmly)* You always have everything first.

Tanya: *(Hands the balloon to Eric and walks away.)*

SCENE 3

Tanya: *(Tosses balloon in the air, having fun by herself.)*

Eric: I want to play with you. *(Tries to join Tanya by tapping balloon up in the air.)*

Tanya: *(Angrily)* No, I had it first, and it's mine.

Eric: *(Angrily)* You always have everything first. I'm not going to play with you anymore if you don't let me play right now.

Tanya: *(Pushes Eric away and yells.)* Go away! I don't want to play with you!

Eric: *(Hits the balloon hard and angrily stomps away.)*

SCENE 4

Tanya: *(Tosses balloon in the air, having fun by herself.)*

Eric: I want to play with you. *(Tries to join Tanya by tapping balloon up in the air.)*

Tanya: *(Angrily)* No, I had it first, and it's mine.

Eric: *(Angrily)* You always have everything first. I'm not going to play with you anymore if you don't let me play right now.

Tanya: *(Pushes Eric away and yells.)* Go away! I don't want to play with you!

Eric: *(Pushes Tanya back.)*

Tanya and Eric: *(Both grab the balloon, which pops.)*

SCENE 5

Tanya: *(Tosses balloon in the air, having fun by herself.)*

Eric: I want to play with you. *(Tries to join Tanya by tapping balloon up in the air.)*

Tanya: I want to play with the balloon by myself.

Eric: Why do you want to play with the balloon by yourself?

Tanya: I'm practicing. This is the first step to learning how to juggle.

Eric: I still want to play with you.

Tanya: I want to play with you, too. I only need to practice a few more minutes. Will you watch and tell me how I'm doing?

Eric: OK. *(Watches Tanya.)* You're good. Will you teach me how to juggle?

Summary: Responses and Outcomes

RESPONSES	OUTCOMES
SOFT	
HARD	
PRINCIPLED	

Understanding Conflict

ORIGINS OF CONFLICT		
LIMITED RESOURCES	**UNMET BASIC NEEDS**	**DIFFERENT VALUES**
Time	Belonging	Beliefs
Money	Power	Priorities
Property	Freedom	Principles
	Fun	

CONFLICT

RESPONSES TO CONFLICT		
SOFT	**HARD**	**PRINCIPLED**
Withdrawing	Threatening	Listening
Ignoring	Pushing	Understanding
Denying	Hitting	Respecting
Giving in	Yelling	Resolving

Sample Conflict Review

INSTRUCTIONS: Think of a conflict you recently had with a friend and tell about it in the boxes below.

WHAT WAS THE CONFLICT?

What happened?

Pete and I were riding bikes. I hit a rock and wiped out. Pete called me a crybaby and mama's boy. I got mad and punched him. We fought.

What did you want?	**What did the other person want?**
I didn't want him to make fun of me. Sympathy.	*I don't know.*

WHAT WERE THE ORIGINS OF THE CONFLICT?		
Resources (time, money, property)	**Basic needs** (belonging, power, freedom, fun)	**Values** (beliefs, priorities, principles)
	To be friends. *Respect.*	*Friends don't bully each other.*

HOW DID YOU RESPOND?		
Soft	**Hard**	**Principled**
	Punched him.	

WHAT WAS THE OUTCOME?		
Lose-Lose	**Win-Lose**	**Win-Win**
We haven't played together since the fight.		

Conflict Review

Think of a conflict you recently had with a friend and tell about it in the boxes below.

WHAT WAS THE CONFLICT?	
What happened?	
What did you want?	**What did the other person want?**

WHAT WERE THE ORIGINS OF THE CONFLICT?		
Resources (time, money, property)	**Basic needs** (belonging, power, freedom, fun)	**Values** (beliefs, priorities, principles)

HOW DID YOU RESPOND?		
Soft	**Hard**	**Principled**

WHAT WAS THE OUTCOME?		
Lose-Lose	**Win-Lose**	**Win-Win**

My Conflicts:
Negative and Positive Outcomes

INSTRUCTIONS: Think of times when conflicts in your life have gone unresolved. Tell about what happened.

_____

_____

_____

_____

_____

_____

INSTRUCTIONS: Think of times when you and other people have worked together to resolve conflicts. Tell about what happened.

_____

_____

_____

_____

_____

_____

Summary: Negative and Positive Outcomes

NEGATIVE (-)

If a conflict remains unresolved, some possible outcomes are:

♦ Threats and blame continue.

♦ Feelings are hurt; relationships are damaged.

♦ Self-interest results; positions harden.

♦ Emotions increase; tempers get out of hand.

♦ Sides are drawn; others get involved.

♦ People do not get what they want and need.

♦ Violence results.

POSITIVE (+)

If people work together for agreement, some possible outcomes are:

♦ Better ideas are produced to solve the problem.

♦ Relationships and communication are improved.

♦ Views are clarified; problems are dealt with.

♦ People listen to and respect one another.

♦ There is cooperation.

♦ People get what they want and need.

♦ Fairness and peace are achieved.

> We have the choice when in conflict to work
> for a positive resolution.

Understanding Peace and Peacemaking

What Peace Means to Me

INSTRUCTIONS: In the boxes write words or draw pictures that come to mind when you think of peace.

PEACE

Definitions of Peace

PEACE is a process of responding to diversity and conflict with tolerance, imagination, and flexibility; war is a product of our intent to stamp out diversity and conflict when we give up on the process of peace. — *George E. Lyon*

PEACE is not a gap between times of fighting, or a space where nothing is happening. Peace is something that lives, spreads, and needs to be looked after. —*Katherine Scholes*

PEACE is that state when each individual fully exercises his or her responsibilities to ensure that all individuals fully enjoy all rights.

PEACE is that state when every individual is able to survive and thrive without being hampered by conflict, prejudice, hatred, antagonism, or injustice.

A Blessing for Peace

One dream: Understand

One hope: Harmony

One prayer: Peace

INSTRUCTIONS: Write your own poem or blessing about peace.

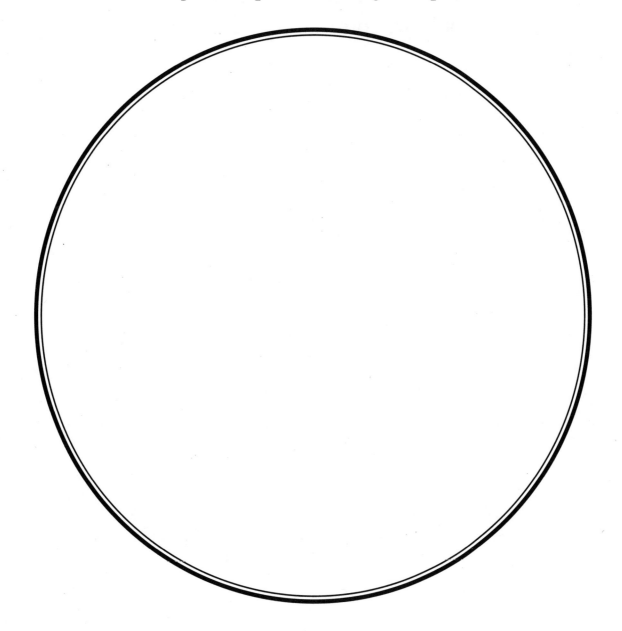

Peacemakers

♦ Peacemakers perceive peace simply as the practice of honoring self, one another, and the environment.

♦ Peacemakers view themselves as responsible for the health, survival, and integrity of the world, whether that world is the classroom, the school, the community, or the earth.

How do you make peace? Peace is made day by day, moment by moment, within each of us and by each of us.

Makers and Breakers

Once upon a time, in a park on a planet far away from Earth, there were beings called Makers and other beings called Breakers. As is often the way in fairy tales, Makers and Breakers were as different as night and day. In fact, Makers played in the park by night, and Breakers played in the park by day. That was the way things were done on this planet. There were daytime beings, and there were nighttime beings. Makers never saw Breakers, and Breakers never saw Makers.

One day, more beings arrived at the planet by spaceship. Silently hovering over the park in their spaceship, they observed both day and night. In the light of day, the spaceship beings watched and listened to the Breakers. They heard raging Breakers yell at one another: *"You can't play! I hate you!" "It's your fault!" "Give me your hat, or I won't play with you!"*

Some of the Breakers wrote hateful messages about other Breakers on the fence that surrounded the park. They tormented one another about being fat, ugly, or stupid. Play fights always ended in vicious real fights. There were Breakers tied to trees being punished for fighting.

Breakers were frenzied. They cut down a tree and blocked the entrance to the park. They hit and kicked one another to get their way. Their games had no rules. Breakers reveled in winning, and they taunted the losers. Many Breakers were alone and angry—they did not laugh and play with others.

When dusk drew near, Breakers pushed and knocked one another over the tree that blocked the way out of the park. Some of the Breakers were hiding under the bushes. They were the last ones to flee the park before it became dark.

Soon after dark, the Makers arrived. It took all of their combined strength to move the huge tree away from the entrance to the park. They cheered loudly to celebrate their feat.

The Makers were kind. They cared about one another, and they cared about the park. They discussed the jobs to be done, and they negotiated to solve disagreements about what would be done and who would do what. Some Makers painted the fence to cover the hateful statements. Other Makers planted trees, bushes, and flowers. Several Makers picked up trash and repaired the broken park benches, swings, and merry-go-round.

When their work was finished, they played. As they played, the spaceship beings heard them say things like *"Thanks for helping me." "That was a great effort you just made! Please keep trying!"* and *"I have a new ball. Will you play with me?"*

There were many games. Everyone followed the rules and helped one another learn new games. Makers encouraged one another, urged one another to try, and praised one another's accomplishments. The Makers painted glow-in-the-dark pictures, danced in the moonlight, and listened to tales about magical fireflies. They shared snacks from their picnic baskets and planned to build a playhouse from the tree that was cut down.

Makers respected one another. They were safe in the park and so was their property—the picnic baskets, jackets, and toys they brought from home.

The spaceship beings were disturbed by what they observed. They had been sent on a mission to live with the Makers and the Breakers. There was not enough room for all of the space beings to play in the nighttime park. The truth was, after watching, no one from the spaceship wanted to play with the Breakers in the daytime.

The spaceship beings pondered the problem:

"During the night the park is filled with peacemakers. They are joyous, creative, and loving. They honor one another and their environment. They know how to resolve conflicts. We witnessed these creatures communicating, inventing, imagining, reflecting, supporting, harmonizing, and calming.

"Peacebreakers dwell in the park in the daytime. They are unhappy, afraid, and hateful. They do not respect one another or their environment. They do not know how to resolve conflicts. We watched these creatures blaming, accusing, frustrating, angering, rejecting, punishing, and withdrawing.

"Each day, peace is broken, and each night, peace is made."

The spaceship beings had learned much about peace by watching the daytime and nighttime park. One morning, the spaceship landed in the park. The spaceship beings had realized what their true mission was. They had been sent to this planet to teach the Breakers how to make peace.

Today and tonight, as it has been ever since the spaceship beings became peacemakers and taught peacemaking behaviors, the park is *peaceable*.

Maker and Breaker Behaviors

INSTRUCTIONS: Write or draw examples of the different kinds of Maker and Breaker behaviors shown in the story.

	PEACEMAKER BEHAVIORS	PEACEBREAKER BEHAVIORS
Doing		
Thinking		
Feeling		

Peacemaking and Peacebreaking: What I See Around Me

INSTRUCTIONS: Write or draw examples of the different kinds of peacemaking and peacebreaking behaviors you see around you.

	PEACEMAKER BEHAVIORS	PEACEBREAKER BEHAVIORS
Doing		
Thinking		
Feeling		

Peacemaking and Peacebreaking: My Behavior

INSTRUCTIONS: Write or draw examples of the different kinds of peacemaking and peacebreaking behaviors you see in yourself.

	PEACEMAKER BEHAVIORS	PEACEBREAKER BEHAVIORS
Doing		
Thinking		
Feeling		

Principles of Conflict Resolution

♦ Separate the people from the problem (perceptions, emotions, communication).

♦ Focus on interests, not positions.

♦ Invent options for mutual gain (**Win-Win** options).

♦ Use fair criteria.

Making Peace

Leah and Elizabeth were neighbors in a high-rise apartment building. Their apartments were next door to each other, and they shared the same balcony. Each day, Leah and Elizabeth would walk to school together, play hopscotch in the park after school, and make peanut butter sandwiches when they got home. They were best friends.

It was Saturday afternoon when Leah decided to have a pretend camping trip on the balcony. She used chairs and blankets to make a tent and her grandmother's quilts to make sleeping bags. Leah knocked on Elizabeth's balcony door and invited her "camping." The girls pretended to fish off the balcony and watched for birds through binoculars, and Leah's mother prepared a campfire in their grill so they could roast hot dogs and marshmallows. The girls thought that this was a wonderful camping trip.

When it was time for bed, Elizabeth ran inside to get her pillow. She came out with her pillow and her kitten. She snuggled into her sleeping bag with her kitten and pillow while Leah was inside brushing her teeth. When Leah returned to the balcony and began to snuggle into her own sleeping bag, the kitten began to meow. Leah yelled, *"Get your kitten out of my tent!"*

Elizabeth said, *"I always sleep with my kitten, and this is my balcony, too!"*

Leah cried, *"Camping was my idea, and I didn't invite your kitten into the tent."*

Elizabeth could see that Leah was really mad, so she closed her eyes and pretended to be asleep. Leah yelled, *"You are not going to be my friend anymore! You're a wimp if you have to sleep with a kitten!"*

Elizabeth stood up and threw the blankets over the balcony. She cried, *"I'm not camping with you if my kitten is not welcome. I'm not going to be your friend. You are too bossy!"*

When Elizabeth started to throw the pillows over the balcony, Leah grabbed her and shoved her down. Elizabeth hit Leah in the face, and they had a terrible fight. Leah and Elizabeth were both crying hysterically, so they barely noticed a dove landing on the rail of the balcony. They were startled when the dove began to speak: *"My, but you girls are certainly disturbing the peace. I am the dove of peace. I am here to teach you the principles of conflict resolution."*

Leah and Elizabeth stared open-mouthed at the dove but quietly listened as the dove continued to speak: *"There are four principles of conflict resolution. If you learn to use these principles, you can make peace.*

"The first principle is to **separate the people from the problem**. Leah, you think Elizabeth is the problem, and, Elizabeth, you think Leah is the problem. The problem is really about the kitten. You each have a different point of view about the kitten's being in the tent. You are angry with each other, and you each probably misunderstand the other. Leah and Elizabeth, if you communicate and understand each other's perceptions and feelings, you will be able to work out the problem about the kitten.

"The second principle," continued the dove, "is to **focus on interests, not positions**. Leah, your position is that the kitten will not sleep in the tent. Elizabeth, your position is that the kitten will sleep in the tent with you."

Then the dove asked Leah, "Leah, why don't you want the kitten to sleep in the tent?"

"Because I'm allergic to cats," Leah said, "and my mother said not to get near any cats."

Then the dove asked Elizabeth, "Elizabeth, why do you want the kitten to sleep in the tent?"

To this Elizabeth replied, "Because my kitten keeps my feet warm, and it's cold out here on the balcony."

So the dove said, "Leah's interest is not getting sick because of her allergy to cats, and Elizabeth's interest is keeping warm. If you focus on interests, then you will find a solution.

"The third principle," the dove went on, "is to **invent options for mutual gain**. These are called Win-Win options. Can you think of possible options that will help both of you?"

Elizabeth said, "I could put my kitten inside and put on more socks."

Then Leah chimed in, "I have some battery-operated warming socks that you can wear, and I have lots of stuffed animals that I can bring out to keep us warm."

"Those are Win-Win options," said the dove, "because they help both of you. They satisfy Elizabeth's interests and Leah's interests.

"The fourth principle," stated the dove, "is to **use fair criteria**. Would it be fair if the solution to the problem made Leah sick? Would it be fair if the solution allowed Elizabeth to be cold? A solution that is fair doesn't allow one to get sick or one to be cold.

"Use these principles to solve your problems, and you will be peacemakers." With those words the dove flew away.

Elizabeth put the kitten to bed inside, and Leah got her battery-operated warming socks and stuffed animals. They retrieved the blankets from underneath the balcony, fixed their tent, and slept peacefully the rest of the night.

Perceptions

**People have problems with perception.
They might say:**

- *"You lied . . . it didn't happen that way."*

- *"I thought of it first."*

- *"You're wrong."*

To deal with problems of perception:

- Put yourself in the other person's shoes.

- Do not blame.

- Try to understand what it feels like to be the other person.

- Try not to make assumptions.

- Discuss perceptions.

We must be careful not to assume that others are wrong or lying if their viewpoints are different.

Emotions

People have problems with emotions:

- ♦ People in conflict often have strong emotions.

- ♦ One person's emotions can provoke another person's emotions.

- ♦ Emotions may interfere with problem solving if they are not acknowledged and understood.

> To make peace we must understand and be able to deal with problems of emotions.

Words to Describe Some Emotions

Happy

Hurt

Excited

Lonely

Annoyed

Anxious

Powerless

Angry

Frustrated

Festive

Comfortable

Embarrassed

Tense

Sad

Peaceful

Courageous

Confused

Furious

Scared

Secure

Terrified

Proud

Joyous

Afraid

Emotional Situations

INSTRUCTIONS: Write the emotions and the possible causes for them in the following situations. *Clue:* Basic needs for *belonging, power, freedom,* and *fun* are often involved in emotional situations.

SITUATION	EMOTION	WHY?
Your aunt just called to say your favorite cousin is coming to spend the weekend.		
You are angry with your best friend because he or she did something with a classmate and you were not asked to join them.		
Your teacher is punishing you for something you believe is not your fault.		
You have just learned that your best friend's father has accepted a job in another state, and the family is moving very soon.		
You have just been notified that your poster was selected to be your school's single entry in the state contest for Earth Day.		

My Anger Situation

INSTRUCTIONS: Think about a recent situation in which you became angry, then fill in the following information.

I was angry with:

_____

What happened:

_____

_____

_____

The other person wanted:

_____

_____

_____

I wanted:

_____

_____

_____

I was angry because:

_____

_____

_____

Rule for Expressing Anger

THE RULE IS . . .

Only one person can express anger at a time.

While the other person vents:

- ♦ Listen.

- ♦ Take deep breaths.

After the other person vents:

- ♦ Say, *"I understand you are angry."*

When emotions are known to both sides,
the people in a conflict are better able to
focus on solving their problem.

Communication Problems

People have problems with communication:

- ♦ They may not be talking to each other.

- ♦ They may not be hearing what the other is saying.

- ♦ They may not be saying what they mean to say.

- ♦ They may be misunderstanding or misinterpreting what they hear.

To help prevent communication problems:

- ♦ Listen actively *(attend, summarize, clarify)*.

- ♦ Send clear messages.

- ♦ Speak to be understood.

- ♦ Speak about yourself.

- ♦ Speak for a purpose.

- ♦ Speak with consideration for the listener.

Active Listening: Attending

**Attending means hearing and understanding.
People know you are listening by your "body talk":**

- ◆ Facial expression

- ◆ Posture

- ◆ Eye contact

- ◆ Gestures

Leaning forward, nodding your head,
and ignoring distractions are ways to show
you are attending.

Active Listening: Summarizing

Summarizing means you state the facts and reflect the feelings. To summarize, you might say:

♦ *"Your Walkman broke when you and Sam collided on the playground. You are mad."*

♦ *"You were sad when you learned that your best friend was moving to a city far away."*

Active Listening: Clarifying

Clarifying means getting additional information to make sure you understand. To clarify, you ask questions:

♦ *"Can you tell me more about _____ ?"*

♦ *"What happened next?"*

♦ *"Is there anything you want to add?"*

♦ *"How would you like this to turn out?"*

♦ *"How would you feel if you were the other person?"*

Communication Inhibitors

Interrupting

Judging

Criticizing

Changing the subject

Joking around

Offering advice

Laughing at others

Bringing up your
own experiences

Sending Clear Messages

♦ Speak to be understood.

♦ Speak about yourself.

♦ Speak for a purpose.

♦ Speak with consideration for the listener.

Focusing on Interests, Not Positions

When there is a conflict, people often make demands or take positions. For example:

    Student A: I want the ball!

    Student B: I want the ball!

    Student A: It's mine. I had it first!

    Student B: It's my turn!

> ## Problems cannot be solved if positions are the focus.

When the focus is on interests, it is possible to solve problems. For example:

    Teacher: Why do you want the ball?

    Student A: To practice dribbling and pass kicks for soccer.

    Teacher: Why do you want the ball?

    Student B: To play and have fun.

You can identify interests by asking: *"Why"* and *"What do you really want?"*

> ## Focusing on interests works because for every interest there will be several possible solutions.

Identifying Positions and Interests

INSTRUCTIONS: Write down the positions and possible interests for each situation. *Clue:* Basic needs for *belonging, power, freedom,* and *fun* are often the interests involved in conflicts.

SITUATION	POSITIONS	INTERESTS
Maria orders Juan, *"Get away from the computer—it's my turn. You have had it a long time, and I need to get my assignment done!"* Juan responds, *"Tough! I signed up for this time, and I'm playing my favorite game. I already finished my work."* Maria goes to tell the teacher.	Maria: Juan:	Maria: Juan:
Keisha yells at LaTasha, *"If you are going to play with Sheila every recess, then you are not my best friend anymore!"* LaTasha replies, *"I want to be your friend, but I also want to play with Sheila and have her be my friend."* LaTasha goes off to play with Sheila.	Keisha: LaTasha:	Keisha: LaTasha:
Brendan is upset with Jeremy: *"Stop putting me down or I won't ever speak to you again!"* Jeremy shouts, *"Big deal! I'm only trying to have a little fun! Lighten up—you never understand when I'm just teasing!"* Brendan stomps away.	Brendan: Jeremy:	Brendan: Jeremy:

SITUATION	POSITIONS	INTERESTS
Linda threatens her younger sister, Dorthea, *"If you ever come into this room again and borrow my stuff without asking, I'm telling Mom!"* Dorthea cries, *"I needed your stuff to make my outfit complete, and you weren't using it. You've borrowed my stuff before!"*	Linda: Dorthea:	Linda: Dorthea:
Gene yells at his friend Peter, *"You can't ride my bike to school anymore. It is never here for me when I need it."* Peter yells, *"I'm riding your bike—you broke my bike."* Peter rides off on the bike.	Gene: Peter:	Gene: Peter:
Marcus says to Tyrone, *"Either buy a lunch or bring your own. I'm tired of sharing my lunch with you!"* Tyrone says, *"You owe me some of your lunch—you ate my candy at recess."* Marcus takes his lunch and moves to another table.	Marcus: Tyrone:	Marcus: Tyrone:

Inventing Options
for Mutual Gain

An option for mutual gain is a suggestion or idea
that addresses the interests of both parties.

These ideas are also called **Win-Win** options.

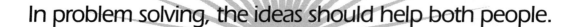

In problem solving, the ideas should help both people.

Rules for Brainstorming

- ♦ Say any idea that comes to mind.

- ♦ Do not judge or discuss ideas.

- ♦ Come up with as many ideas as possible.

- ♦ Try to think of unusual ideas.

In brainstorming, people focus only on
generating ideas, not on deciding whether
the ideas are good or bad.

Using Fair Criteria

INSTRUCTIONS: In the boxes write words or draw pictures that come to mind when you think of fairness.

FAIRNESS

Using fair criteria means to judge:
Without self-interest, but with mutual interest
Without prejudice, but with respect
Without emotion, but with reason

Mediation

Mediation

Mediation is a communication process in which a third party helps people work together to resolve conflicts peaceably.

THE MEDIATOR HELPS THOSE IN CONFLICT . . .

♦ Focus on the problem and not blame the other person.

♦ Understand and respect different views.

♦ Communicate wants and feelings.

♦ Cooperate in solving a problem.

Mediators are peacemakers.

Role of the Mediator

THE MEDIATOR . . .

- ♦ Is impartial (does not take sides).

- ♦ Listens with empathy.

- ♦ Is respectful.

- ♦ Is trustworthy.

- ♦ Helps people work together.

The mediator builds trust and cooperation,
making mutual problem solving possible.

Steps in the Mediation Process

- ♦ **Step 1:** Agree to Mediate

- ♦ **Step 2:** Gather Points of View

- ♦ **Step 3:** Focus on Interests

- ♦ **Step 4:** Create Win-Win Options

- ♦ **Step 5:** Evaluate Options

- ♦ **Step 6:** Create an Agreement

Sample Mediation

STEP 1: AGREE TO MEDIATE

Hannah: *Welcome to mediation. My name is Hannah.*

Drake: *My name is Drake. We are your mediators. What are your names?*

Antonio: My name is Antonio.

Joe: My name is Joe.

Hannah: *The rules of mediation are: Mediators do not take sides, take turns talking and listening—so don't interrupt each other—and cooperate to solve the problem. Are you willing to follow these rules?*

Joe: OK.

Antonio: Yes!

STEP 2: GATHER POINTS OF VIEW

Drake: *Antonio, please tell what happened.*

Antonio: Well, I was getting the last basketball out of the ball bin. I got there first. While I was asking some friends to play with me, Joe came along and tried to take the ball. He said he should get to play with the ball because he always does.

Drake: *You were getting the last basketball to play with some friends, and Joe tried to take the ball. He wanted to play with the ball like he always does.*

Antonio: Yeah . . . that's what he did.

Drake: *Joe, please tell your point of view.*

Joe: Well, it was my ball because I always play with it. That is all I want to say.

Drake: *Joe, you believe the ball was yours because you always play with it. Antonio, how did you feel when that happened?*

Antonio: I was mad. He was being a bully. That's why we got into a fight.

Drake: *You were mad and got in a fight with Joe. Do you have anything to add?*

Antonio: No.

Drake: *Joe, do you have anything to add?*

Joe: I wanted the ball, and I fought Antonio for it. He never lets me play on his team.

Drake: *You never get to play on Antonio's team, and you fought Antonio for the last ball.*

STEP 3: FOCUS ON INTERESTS

Hannah: *Antonio, what do you want?*

Antonio: I want to play basketball with my friends.

Hannah: *Joe, what do you want?*

Joe: If there is only one ball left, I want it.

Hannah: *Why do you want the ball?*

Joe: I want to play basketball.

Hannah: *Well, you both want the same thing. You want to play basketball.*

Antonio: Yes.

Joe: Yes.

Hannah: *So what's going to happen if you don't reach an agreement?*

Antonio: Well, I think we'll be rushing out early to try to get the ball from each other and end up in the principal's office again for fighting.

Hannah: *So you're saying if you don't solve the problem, you're both going to be rushing out to get the ball and probably fight again.*

Antonio: Yes.

Hannah: *Joe, do you have anything to say about that?*

Joe: Well, I think if we don't find an agreement we'll just always be arguing about who gets the ball and never get to play.

Hannah: *How would you feel if you were the other person?*

Antonio: I might feel left out. I didn't know Joe wanted to play on my team.

Joe: I would be happy to play on a team with my friends.

Hannah: *Both of you seem to want to reach an agreement so you don't fight over the ball. Both of you want to play basketball and be on a team with friends.*

STEP 4: CREATE WIN-WIN OPTIONS

Drake: *Now it's time to create Win-Win options. We use brainstorming rules to create options. You may say any idea that comes to mind, but do not judge or discuss ideas at this time. Try to come up with as many ideas as possible, and try to think of unusual ideas. OK, suggest ideas that will help both of you.*

Antonio: Well, if we took turns—like one time he could get it, and then one time I could get it. We could keep going like that.

Joe: Well, I think that if there is only one ball left, we should just share it and play ball together.

Drake: *Remember to think of unusual ideas.*

Antonio: We could organize a team sign-up sheet.

Joe: We could have a tournament.

Antonio: We could ask the principal to buy more basketballs.

Joe: We could play indoor soccer. More people can play soccer.

Drake: *Can you think of anything else to do?*

Joe: Not right now.

Antonio: Me, either.

STEP 5: EVALUATE OPTIONS

Hannah: *OK, let's think about all the options. Do you think any of these will work?*

Antonio: I don't think the principal is going to buy more balls.

Joe: I don't think so either. I think it would be hard keeping track of taking turns and remembering who had the ball last.

Antonio: Yeah, we might fight over whose turn it was to play with the ball. It would work to play basketball together.

Hannah: *Can you combine options?*

Joe: We could combine the team sign-up with the tournament.

Antonio: We probably need to ask the principal if that would be all right.

Hannah: *Is playing basketball together and asking the principal about team sign-up and a tournament a fair solution?*

Antonio: It's fair.

Joe: Yes, I think so.

STEP 6: CREATE AN AGREEMENT

Drake: *How will you do it?*

Antonio: We could play basketball together tomorrow.

Drake: *When?*

Antonio: We could play at lunchtime.

Drake: *What is your plan for the sign-up and tournament?*

Joe: We can talk to the principal after school today. If he says yes, we can make the sign-up sheets for the teams and put together the tournament.

Drake: *Antonio, what have you agreed to do?*

Antonio: I have agreed to play basketball with Joe tomorrow at lunchtime and to go with Joe to talk with the principal about the team sign-up and the tournament.

Drake: *Joe, what have you agreed to do?*

Joe: I will play basketball with Antonio tomorrow at lunch and go with him to talk to the principal, and make the team sign-up and put the tournament together if it's OK.

Antonio: I'll help with sign-up and tournament, too!

(Hannah and Drake shake hands with Antonio and Joe.)

Drake: *Do you want to shake hands?*

(Antonio and Joe shake hands.)

Step 1: Agree to Mediate

♦ **Welcome both people and introduce yourself as the mediator.**

♦ **Explain the ground rules:**

Mediators do not take sides.

Take turns talking and listening.

Cooperate to solve the problem.

♦ **Ask each person:**

"Are you willing to follow the rules?"

The mediation rules help make the process fair.

Red Riding Hood and the Wolf

Tasha: *Hello, I am Tasha and this is Shawn. We are your mediators. What is your name?*

Red: I'm Red Riding Hood. They used to call me Little Red Riding Hood, but they don't anymore. You see, the Wolf and I have had this problem a long time, and I grew up.

Tasha: *What is your name?*

Wolf: I'm the Wolf.

Tasha: *Welcome to mediation. I'm sorry it took you so long to find us. The rules that make mediation work are as follows: Mediators do not take sides. You take turns talking and listening. You cooperate to solve the problem. Red Riding Hood, do you agree to the rules?*

Red: Yes.

Tasha: *Wolf, do you agree to the rules?*

Wolf: Yes, I do.

Shawn: *Red Riding Hood, please tell what happened.*

Red: Well, you see, I was taking a loaf of fresh bread and some cakes to my granny's cottage on the other side of the woods. Granny wasn't well, so I thought I would pick some flowers for her along the way.

I was picking the flowers when the Wolf jumped out from behind a tree and started asking me a bunch of questions. He wanted to know what I was doing and where I was going, and he kept grinning this wicked grin and smacking his lips together.

He was being so gross and rude. Then he ran away.

Shawn: *You were taking some food to your grandmother on the other side of the woods, and the Wolf appeared from behind a tree and frightened you.*

Red: Yes, that's what happened.

Shawn: *Wolf, please tell what happened.*

Wolf: The forest is my home. I care about it and try to keep it clean. One day, when I was cleaning up some garbage that people had left behind, I heard footsteps. I leaped behind a tree and saw a girl coming down the trail carrying a basket.

I was suspicious because she was dressed in this strange red cape with her head covered up as if she didn't want anyone to know who she was. She started picking my flowers and stepping on my new little pine trees.

Naturally, I stopped to ask her what she was doing and all that. She gave me this song and dance about going to her granny's house with a basket of goodies.

Shawn: *You were concerned when you saw this girl dressed in red picking your flowers. You stopped her and asked her what she was doing.*

Wolf: That's right.

Shawn: *Red Riding Hood, is there anything you want to add?*

Red: Yes. When I got to my granny's house, the Wolf was disguised in my granny's nightgown. He tried to eat me with those big ugly teeth. I'd be dead today if it hadn't been for a woodsman who came in and saved me. The Wolf scared my granny. I found her hiding under the bed.

Shawn: *You are saying the Wolf put on your granny's nightgown so you would think he was your granny and that he tried to hurt you?*

Red: I said he tried to *eat* me.

Shawn: *So you felt he was trying to eat you. Wolf, do you have anything to add?*

Wolf: Of course I do. I know this girl's granny. I thought we should teach Red Riding Hood a lesson for prancing on my pine trees in that get-up and for picking my flowers. I let her go on her way, but I ran ahead to her granny's cottage.

When I saw Granny I explained what happened, and she agreed her granddaughter needed to learn a lesson. Granny hid under the bed, and I dressed up in her nightgown.

When Red Riding Hood came into the bedroom, she saw me in the bed and said something nasty about my big ears. I've been told my ears are big before, so I tried to make the best of it by saying my big ears help me hear her better.

Then she made an insulting crack about my bulging eyes. This one was really hard to blow off because she sounded so nasty. Still, I make it a policy to turn the other cheek, so I told her my big eyes help me see her better.

Her next insult about my big teeth really got to me. You see, I'm quite sensitive about them. I know when she made fun of my teeth I should have had better control, but I leaped from the bed and growled that my teeth would help me to eat her.

Shawn: *So you and Granny tried to play a trick on Red Riding Hood to teach her a lesson. Explain more about the eating part.*

Wolf: Now, let's face it. Everyone knows no wolf could ever eat a girl, but crazy Red Riding Hood started screaming and running around the house. I tried to catch her to calm her down.

All of a sudden the door came crashing open, and a big woodsman stood there with his ax. I knew I was in trouble . . . there was an open window behind me, so out I went.

I've been hiding ever since. There are terrible rumors going around the forest about me. Red Riding Hood is calling me the Big Bad Wolf. I'd like to say I've gotten over feeling bad, but the truth is I haven't lived happily ever after.

I don't understand why Granny never told my side of the story.

Shawn: *You're upset about the rumors and have been afraid to show your face in the forest. You're also confused about why Granny hasn't set things straight and has let the situation go on for this long.*

Wolf: It just isn't fair. I'm miserable and lonely.

Shawn: *Red Riding Hood, would you tell us more about Granny?*

Red: Well, Granny has been sick—and she's been very tired lately. When I asked her how she came to be under the bed, she said she couldn't remember a thing that had happened.

Step 2: Gather Points of View

♦ **Say:**

"Please tell what happened."

♦ **Listen, summarize, clarify. To clarify, ask:**

"How did you feel when that happened?"

"Do you have anything to add?"

In this step, the disputants hear each
other's perceptions and emotions.

Step 3: Focus on Interests

♦ **Ask:**

"What do you want?"

"Why?"

♦ **Listen, summarize, clarify. To clarify, ask:**

"What might happen if you don't reach an agreement?"

"Why has the other person not done what you wanted?"

"What would you think if you were in the other person's shoes?"

♦ **Summarize the interests. Say:**

"Your interests are _____ ."

Shared and compatible interests are the
building blocks of the resolution. Most common
interests are associated with the basic needs
for belonging, power, freedom, and fun.

Step 4: Create Win-Win Options

♦ **Explain the brainstorming rules:**

Say any idea that comes to mind.

Do not judge or discuss ideas.

Come up with as many ideas
as possible.

Try to think of unusual ideas.

♦ **Say:**

*"Please suggest ideas that address
the interests of both of you."*

*"Can you think of more possibilities
that will help both of you?"*

The mediator remembers the ideas
presented by the disputants.

Step 5: Evaluate Options

♦ **Ask:**

"Can you combine options or parts of options?"

♦ **For each option, ask:**

"Is this option fair?"

"Can you do it?"

"Do you think it will work?"

In this step, the disputants become side-by-side problem solvers in evaluating options.

Step 6: Create an Agreement

♦ **Ask disputants to make a plan of action:**

   "Who, what, when, where, and how?"

♦ **Ask each person to summarize the plan.**

♦ **Ask:**

   "Is the problem solved?"

♦ **Shake hands with each person.**

♦ **Ask:**

   *"Do you want to shake hands
   with each other?"*

Because the problem is between the disputants,
the agreement must be their agreement—
something they both will do. The agreement
is often a combination of ideas.

The Peaceable School Mediation Process

STEP 1: AGREE TO MEDIATE

♦ Welcome both people and introduce yourself as the mediator.

♦ Explain the ground rules:

Mediators do not take sides.

Take turns talking and listening.

Cooperate to solve the problem.

♦ Ask each person: *"Are you willing to follow the rules?"*

STEP 2: GATHER POINTS OF VIEW

♦ Say: *"Please tell what happened."*

♦ Listen, summarize, clarify. To clarify, ask:

"How did you feel when that happened?"

"Do you have anything to add?"

STEP 3: FOCUS ON INTERESTS

♦ Ask:

"What do you want?"

"Why?"

♦ Listen, summarize, clarify. To clarify, ask:

"What might happen if you don't reach an agreement?"

"Why has the other person not done what you wanted?"

"What would you think if you were in the other person's shoes?"

♦ Summarize the interests. Say: *"Your interests are _____."*

STEP 4: CREATE WIN-WIN OPTIONS

♦ Explain the brainstorming rules:

Say any idea that comes to mind.

Do not judge or discuss ideas.

Come up with as many ideas as possible.

Try to think of unusual ideas.

♦ Say:

"Please suggest ideas that address the interests of both of you."

"Can you think of more possibilities that will help both of you?"

STEP 5: EVALUATE OPTIONS

♦ Ask: *"Can you combine options or parts of options?"*

♦ For each option, ask:

"Is this option fair?"

"Can you do it?"

"Do you think it will work?"

STEP 6: CREATE AN AGREEMENT

♦ Ask disputants to make a plan of action:
"Who, what, when, where, and how?"

♦ Ask each person to summarize the plan.

♦ Ask: *"Is the problem solved?"*

♦ Shake hands with each person.

♦ Ask: *"Do you want to shake hands with each other?"*

Negotiation

Negotiation

Negotiation is a communication process allowing people to work together to resolve their conflicts peaceably.

THE NEGOTIATOR WORKS TO . . .

♦ Focus on the problem and not blame the other person.

♦ Understand and respect different points of view.

♦ Communicate wants and feelings.

♦ Cooperate in solving a problem.

Negotiators are peacemakers.

Role of the Negotiator

THE NEGOTIATOR . . .

♦ Listens with empathy.

♦ Suspends judgment.

♦ Is respectful.

♦ Has a cooperative spirit.

The negotiator builds trust and cooperation,
making mutual problem solving possible.

Steps in the Negotiation Process

♦ **Step 1:** Agree to Negotiate

♦ **Step 2:** Gather Points of View

♦ **Step 3:** Focus on Interests

♦ **Step 4:** Create Win-Win Options

♦ **Step 5:** Evaluate Options

♦ **Step 6:** Create an Agreement

Sample Negotiation

STEP 1: AGREE TO NEGOTIATE

Ruthie: I agree to take turns talking and listening, and I agree to cooperate to solve the problem.

Cierra: I agree to cooperate to solve the problem. I agree to take turns talking and listening. Do you want to talk first?

STEP 2: GATHER POINTS OF VIEW

Ruthie: OK. I shoved your books off the table. I was angry because I think you stole my colored pencils. You were using colored pencils, and I can't find mine.

Cierra: So you think I stole your colored pencils because you can't find yours. You were angry and shoved my books off the table because you thought I was using your pencils.

Ruthie: Yes.

Cierra: Well, my point of view is I was coloring with the pencils my aunt gave me for my birthday. I was mad when you shoved my books off the table, so I shoved your chair and you fell. I feel hurt when you accuse me of stealing your stuff.

Ruthie: Your point of view is that you were using colored pencils your aunt gave you. You were mad when I shoved your books, so you shoved my chair. You feel hurt when I accuse you of stealing.

Cierra: Yes, that's my point of view.

STEP 3: FOCUS ON INTERESTS

Ruthie: I want my colored pencils because I need to use them for the poster project and I like to draw with them.

Cierra: You want your colored pencils because you need them for the project and you like drawing with them.

Ruthie: Yes.

Cierra: I want you to stop accusing me of stealing because that hurts. I don't steal. I want to be your friend because I like you.

Ruthie: You want me to stop accusing you of stealing because it hurts. You don't steal, and you want to be my friend.

STEP 4: CREATE WIN-WIN OPTIONS

Cierra: What are some options that could help us?

Ruthie: I could stop accusing you of stealing and ask if you have seen my stuff.

Cierra: I could help you find your colored pencils, or you could use mine for the poster project if we haven't found yours.

Ruthie: I could ask the teacher to help us look for them.

Cierra: We could make a lost-and-found box and put a notice on it that your pencils are lost. That way the whole class can help find them.

Ruthie: We could work together on the poster project and help each other.

Cierra: We could put signs up all over the school about your missing pencils.

STEP 5: EVALUATE OPTIONS

Ruthie: It would be fair if I stopped accusing you of stealing every time I'm missing something. I could ask you if you have seen my stuff. I can do that.

Cierra: I think that's fair.

Ruthie: We could look for my pencils together and share your pencils when we work together on the poster project if we don't find mine right away.

Cierra: I think the lost-and-found box will really work.

Ruthie: Me, too. We can ask the teacher if that's OK. That way she won't need to help us look.

Cierra: We can do that together.

Ruthie: I never take my pencils out of class, so I don't think we need to put signs up all over the school.

Cierra: I think these options are fair. They cover both our interests.

STEP 6: CREATE AN AGREEMENT

Ruthie: Let's make a plan.

Cierra: OK. We can talk to the teacher about the lost-and-found box at recess this afternoon.

Ruthie: We can make the lost-and-found box today after school.

Cierra: We can look together for the pencils at lunchtime.

Ruthie: We could work on the poster project on Saturday morning at my house even if we do find my pencils.

Cierra: What if you forget and accuse me of stealing again?

Ruthie: You could remind me to ask you. OK?

Cierra: OK.

Ruthie: I don't think I'll forget.

Cierra: OK, if you accuse me of stealing, I have agreed to remind you to ask me. I have agreed to look for your pencils with you at lunchtime, talk with the teacher at recess, make the lost-and-found box after school, and work on the poster project with you on Saturday. We can use my pencils if we don't find yours.

Ruthie: I have agreed to stop accusing you of stealing, to look for my pencils at lunchtime, to go with you and talk with the teacher at recess, to make the lost-and-found box, and to work together on the poster project on Saturday.

(Ruthie and Cierra shake hands.)

Step 1: Agree to Negotiate

♦ **Say:**

"I agree to take turns talking and listening."

"I agree to cooperate to solve the problem."

The negotiation rules help make the process fair.

Red Riding Hood and the Wolf: Gather Points of View

Red: I'm Red Riding Hood. I agree to take turns talking and listening and to cooperate to solve the problem.

Wolf: I'm the Wolf. I agree to take turns talking and listening, and I agree to cooperate with you, Red Riding Hood, to solve the problem.

Red: I was taking a loaf of fresh bread and some cakes to my granny's cottage on the other side of the woods. Granny wasn't well, so I thought I would pick some flowers for her along the way.

I was picking the flowers when you, Wolf, jumped out from behind a tree and started asking me a bunch of questions. You wanted to know what I was doing and where I was going, and you kept grinning that wicked grin and smacking your lips together. You were being so gross and rude. Then you ran away. I was frightened.

Wolf: You were taking some food to your grandmother on the other side of the woods, and I appeared from behind the tree and frightened you.

Red: Yes, that's what happened.

Wolf: Well, look, Red, the forest is my home. I care about it and try to keep it clean. That day, I was cleaning up some garbage people had left behind when I heard footsteps. I leaped behind a tree and saw you coming down the trail carrying a basket.

I was suspicious because you were dressed in that strange red cape with your head covered up as if you didn't want anyone to know who you were. You started picking my flowers and stepping on my new little pine trees.

Naturally, I stopped to ask you what you were doing. You gave me this song and dance about going to your granny's house with a basket of goodies.

I wasn't very happy about the way you treated my home or me.

Red: You were concerned when you saw me in a red cape picking your flowers. You stopped me and asked me what I was doing.

Wolf: That's right.

Red: Well, the problem didn't stop there. When I got to my granny's house, you were disguised in my granny's nightgown. You tried to eat me with those big ugly teeth. I'd be dead today if it hadn't been for the woodsman who came in and saved me. You scared my granny. I found her hiding under the bed.

Wolf: You say I put on your granny's nightgown so you would think I was your granny, and that I tried to hurt you?

Red: I said you tried to *eat* me. I really thought you were going to eat me up. I was hysterical.

Wolf: Now wait a minute, Red. I know your granny. I thought we should teach you a lesson for prancing on my pine trees in that get-up and for picking my flowers. I let you go on your way in the woods, but I ran ahead to your granny's cottage.

When I saw Granny, I explained what happened, and she agreed that you needed to learn a lesson. Granny hid under the bed, and I dressed up in her nightgown.

When you came into the bedroom you saw me in the bed and said something nasty about my big ears. I've been told my ears are big before, so I tried to make the best of it by saying big ears help me hear you better.

Then you made an insulting crack about my bulging eyes. This one was really hard to blow off, because you sounded so nasty. Still, I make it a policy to turn the other cheek, so I told you my big eyes help me see you better.

Your next insult about my big teeth really got to me. You see, I'm quite sensitive about my teeth. I know that when you made fun of my teeth I should have had better control, but I leaped from the bed and growled that my teeth would help me to eat you.

But, come on, Red! Let's face it. Everyone knows no wolf could ever eat a girl, but you started screaming and running around the house. I tried to catch you to calm you down.

All of a sudden the door came crashing open, and a big woodsman stood there with his ax. I knew I was in trouble . . . there was an open window behind me, so out I went.

I've been hiding ever since. There are terrible rumors going around the forest about me. Red, you called me the Big Bad Wolf. I'd like to say I've gotten over feeling bad, but the truth is I haven't lived happily ever after.

I don't understand why Granny never told you and the others my side of the story. I'm upset about the rumors and have been afraid to show my face in the forest. Why have you and Granny let the situation go on for this long? It just isn't fair. I'm miserable and lonely.

Red: You think that I have started unfair rumors about you, and you are miserable and lonely and don't understand why Granny didn't tell your side of the story.

Well, Granny has been sick—and she's been very tired lately. When I asked her how she came to be under the bed, she said she couldn't remember a thing that had happened. Come to think of it, she didn't seem too upset . . . just confused.

Wolf: So you think it is possible that Granny just doesn't remember because she is sick.

Step 2: Gather Points of View

STUDENT A

- ◆ **Tell your view of the problem. Say:**

    "I was _____ ." (Tell what you were doing.)

    "I feel _____ ."

STUDENT B

- ◆ **Listen and summarize Student A's view of the problem.**

- ◆ **Tell your view of the problem. Say:**

    "I was _____ ." (Tell what you were doing.)

    "I feel _____ ."

STUDENT A

- ◆ **Listen and summarize Student B's view of the problem.**

- ◆ **Clarify by adding anything more about your point of view.**

STUDENT B

- ◆ **Listen and summarize what Student A adds.**

- ◆ **Clarify by adding anything more about your point of view.**

STUDENT A

- ◆ **Listen and summarize what Student B adds.**

Remember to put yourself in the other person's shoes.

Red Riding Hood and the Wolf: Focus on Interests

Red: I want to be able to take flowers to Granny when I visit her because she is lonely and flowers help cheer her up.

I want to be able to go through the forest to Granny's house because it is too far to take the road around the forest.

I want you to stop trying to scare me or threaten me in the forest because I want to feel safe. Besides, I think the forest is a fun place.

Wolf: You want to go through the forest to visit Granny, who is lonely, and you want to feel safe because you think the forest is a neat place.

Red: Yes, and I want to take flowers to Granny.

Wolf: I want you to watch where you are walking and to stop picking my flowers because I want to keep my forest home looking nice.

I want the rumors to stop because I want people to like me, and I want to be able to enjoy the forest without being afraid that someone is hunting for me.

Red: You want the forest to be pretty, you want people who visit the forest to like you and not be afraid of you, and you want to be safe in the forest.

Wolf: Right, the forest is my home. I should be free to enjoy my own home.

Step 3: Focus on Interests

♦ **Say what you want and why:**

   "I want ____ because ____."

♦ **Listen, summarize, clarify. To clarify, ask:**

   *"What will happen if we do not
   solve the problem?"*

   *"What would you think if you
   were in my shoes?"*

Shared and compatible interests are
the building blocks of the resolution. Most
interests are associated with the basic needs
for belonging, power, freedom, and fun.

Red Riding Hood and the Wolf: Create Win-Win Options

Red: In order to solve this problem, I could try to stay on the path when I walk through the forest.

Wolf: I could try to remember to call out when I hear you coming instead of quietly stepping out from behind a tree. I could plant some flowers over by Granny's house for you to pick.

Red: I could pick up trash I see in the forest and take it to Granny's trash can.

Wolf: I could check up on Granny to make sure she is OK on those days when you can't make it. She is my friend, you see.

Red: Granny and I can talk to the woodsman and tell him we made a mistake about you. I could tell my friends that I'm not afraid of you anymore—that you can be nice.

Wolf: I could meet your friends on the edge of the forest and show them through it.

Step 4: Create Win-Win Options

♦ **Invent at least three options to address the interests of both of you.**

♦ **Follow the brainstorming rules:**

Say any idea that comes to mind.

Do not judge or discuss ideas.

Come up with as many ideas as possible.

Try to think of unusual ideas.

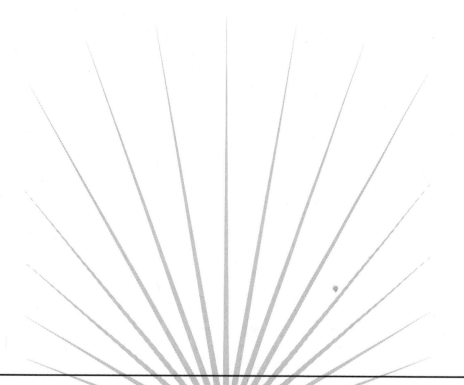

Negotiators keep track of the options generated.

Red Riding Hood and the Wolf: Evaluate Options

Wolf: Do you think if you tell the woodsman and your friends that you made a mistake about me and that I'm really nice, then I won't have to worry about the woodsman and his hunters catching me?

Red: I think that will work.

Wolf: Maybe I could go with you to talk to the woodsman.

Red: Yes, that would help. You could also go with me when I tell my friends I'm not afraid of you anymore . . . I'd like to help you plant some flowers at Granny's, and I could also help you plant some in the forest. It would be nice to visit Granny together. She's pretty lonely.

Wolf: That sounds good.

Red: I agree.

Wolf: I don't think it will work for you to stay on the path all the time. I can show you where to walk so you don't harm anything.

Red: I think that's fair.

Wolf: I agree.

Red: Will it work for you to check on Granny when I can't visit her?

Wolf: Yes, if you call me early in the morning.

Red: I think it would be a good idea if I ask my friends for a donation when you give them a tour of the forest, and we could use the money to buy more trees to plant and start a recycling program for the trash we pick up.

Wolf: I think we've taken care of both of our interests.

Red: This solution will help both of us.

Step 5: Evaluate Options

◆ **Combine options or parts of options.**

◆ **For each option, work together to decide:**

"Is this option fair?"

"Can we do it?"

"Do we think it will work?"

In this step, negotiators become side-by-side
problem solvers in evaluating options.

Red Riding Hood and the Wolf: Create an Agreement

Red: I'll arrange for Granny and myself to talk to the woodsman. I'll try to get an appointment for this afternoon, and I'll let you know when.

Wolf: I'll get some flowers to plant at Granny's. I'll have them ready to plant by Saturday. I'll draw up a possible forest tour map and give it to you.

Red: As soon as I get your tour map, I'll bring some friends over to try it out. That's when I'll introduce you and tell them you're nice.

Wolf: I'll put a donations box at the edge of the forest for our tree planting and recycling program.

Red: And I'll call you by 7 o'clock if I can't go visit Granny.

Wolf: OK. I've agreed to get flowers to plant by Saturday, to draw a tour map of the forest, to go along with you to talk with the woodsman, to meet your friends and lead a tour through the forest, to take care of the donations box, and to visit Granny when you can't do it.

Red: I've agreed to arrange for an appointment with Granny and the woodsman, to plant flowers with you, to bring my friends to tour the forest and introduce you as a nice wolf, and to call you by 7 o'clock if I can't visit Granny.

(The two shake hands.)

Step 6: Create an Agreement

♦ **Make a plan of action:**

  "Who, what, when, where, and how?"

♦ **Summarize what you have agreed to do. Say:**

  "I have agreed to _____."

♦ **Shake hands**.

The agreement is often a combination of ideas.
It must be something both people will do.

The Peaceable School Negotiation Process

STEP 1: AGREE TO NEGOTIATE

♦ Say:

"I agree to take turns talking and listening."

"I agree to cooperate to solve the problem."

STEP 2: GATHER POINTS OF VIEW

STUDENT A

♦ Tell your view of the problem. Say:

"I was _____ ." (Tell what you were doing.)

"I feel _____ ."

STUDENT B

♦ Listen and summarize Student A's view of the problem.

♦ Tell your view of the problem. Say:

"I was _____ ." (Tell what you were doing.)

"I feel _____ ."

STUDENT A

♦ Listen and summarize Student B's view of the problem.

♦ Clarify by adding anything more about your point of view.

STUDENT B

♦ Listen and summarize what Student A adds.

♦ Clarify by adding anything more about your point of view.

STUDENT A

♦ Listen and summarize what Student B adds.

STEP 3: FOCUS ON INTERESTS

♦ Say what you want and why: *"I want ——— because ———."*

♦ Listen, summarize, clarify. To clarify, ask:

"What will happen if we do not solve the problem?"

"What would you think if you were in my shoes?"

STEP 4: CREATE WIN-WIN OPTIONS

♦ Invent at least three options to address the interests of both of you.

♦ Follow the brainstorming rules:

Say any idea that comes to mind.

Do not judge or discuss ideas.

Come up with as many ideas as possible.

Try to think of unusual ideas.

STEP 5: EVALUATE OPTIONS

♦ Combine options or parts of options.

♦ For each option, work together to decide:

"Is this option fair?"

"Can we do it?"

"Do we think it will work?"

STEP 6: CREATE AN AGREEMENT

♦ Make a plan of action: *"Who, what, when, where, and how?"*

♦ Summarize what you have agreed to do.
Say: *"I have agreed to ———."*

♦ Shake hands.

Group Problem Solving

Find Someone Who...

INSTRUCTIONS: Find someone in the group who fits each of the following statements. Have the person sign his or her name by the statement.

Is left-handed   _____

Likes rap music   _____

Is good at math   _____

Has a pierced ear   _____

Has braces or a retainer   _____

Plays a musical instrument   _____

Has a parent who was born in a foreign country   _____

Plays on a sports team   _____

Has black hair   _____

Is good at art   _____

Is a cat lover   _____

Likes to fish   _____

Has allergies   _____

Has freckles   _____

Likes to skateboard or rollerblade   _____

Sentence Completions

INSTRUCTIONS: Here are some sentences about you. Please finish them with the first thought that comes to your mind.

I like to:	**I am best at:**
One word that describes me is:	**I sometimes wish:**
I worry when:	**I am afraid of:**
I hate to hear people say:	**I get angry when:**

Group Problem Solving

Group problem solving is a communication process for helping people work together to resolve conflicts. Group problem solving follows two main guidelines:

◆ The discussion is always directed toward solving the problem.

◆ The solution never includes punishment or fault finding.

THE GROUP PROBLEM SOLVER WORKS TO . . .

◆ Understand and respect different points of view.

◆ Focus on the problem and not blame others.

◆ Communicate wants and feelings.

◆ Cooperate to solve the problem.

Group problem solvers are peacemakers.

Role of the Group Problem Solver

THE GROUP PROBLEM SOLVER . . .

- ◆ Listens with empathy.

- ◆ Suspends judgment.

- ◆ Is respectful.

- ◆ Has a cooperative spirit.

The group problem solver builds
trust and cooperation.

Ground Rules for
Group Problem Solving

♦ **Participants sit in a circle.**

♦ **Every member of the class is responsible for communication** *(listening and speaking).* This means that each member is responsible for sharing his or her point of view about the problem if it has not already been shared by another.

♦ **The** *"Rule of Focus"* **applies to all discussion.** This means that whoever is speaking will be allowed to talk without being interrupted.

♦ **Participants show respect for others.** This means no criticism or sarcasm toward group members or their ideas.

♦ **Each time someone in the group finishes making a statement, another group member summarizes and clarifies it before anyone else goes on to a new idea.**

Steps in the Group-Problem-Solving Process

♦ **Step 1:** Agree to Problem Solve

♦ **Step 2:** Gather Points of View

♦ **Step 3:** Focus on Interests in the Group

♦ **Step 4:** Create Win-Win Options

♦ **Step 5a:** Establish Criteria to Evaluate Options

♦ **Step 5b:** Evaluate Options

♦ **Step 6:** Create an Agreement

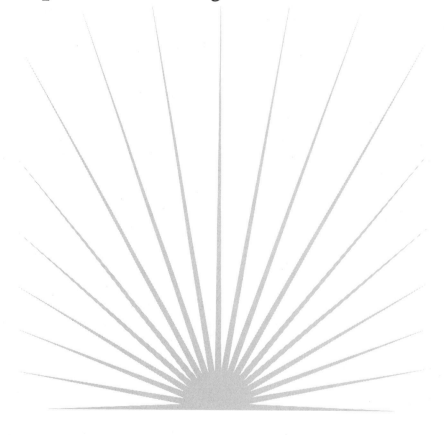

Step 1: Agree to Problem Solve

♦ **Listen for the purpose of the meeting.**

♦ **Follow the group-problem-solving rules:**

Participants sit in a circle.

Every member of the class is responsible for communication *(listening and speaking)*. This means that each member is responsible for sharing his or her point of view about the problem if it has not already been shared by another.

The *"Rule of Focus"* applies to all discussion. This means that whoever is speaking will be allowed to talk without being interrupted.

Participants show respect for others. This means no criticism or sarcasm toward group members or their ideas.

Each time someone in the group finishes making a statement, another group member summarizes and clarifies it before anyone else goes on to a new idea.

♦ **Listen for and think about any special rules for this particular meeting.**

Step 2: Gather Points of View

♦ **Participate in the discussion** *(listen and speak)*.

♦ **Tell what you know and how you feel about the problem:**

Speak to be understood.

Do not place blame.

Speak if your point of view has not already been stated by another group member.

♦ **Help the group decide on the problem statement. The problem statement tells exactly what problem you are trying to solve.**

Group members hear one another's perceptions and emotions.

Step 3: Focus on Interests in the Group

♦ **Tell what you want in the situation and why you want what you want.**

♦ **If you don't know what you want and why:**

Tell why you think the problem is not going away.

Tell what you think is likely to happen if the group cannot agree on a solution.

Group members' shared and compatible interests are the building blocks of the resolution.

Step 4: Create Win-Win Options

♦ **Suggest ideas that will address the interests of group members.**

♦ **Follow the brainstorming rules:**

Say any idea that comes to mind.

Do not judge or discuss ideas.

Come up with as many ideas as possible.

Try to think of unusual ideas.

Step 5a: Establish Criteria to Evaluate Options

♦ **Decide what criteria are important to consider. For example:**

Does the option follow our school's rights and responsibilities?

Does the option help everyone involved?

Is the option fair?

Can the option solve the problem?

Can the group do it?

Criteria are the standards you use to decide whether or not an option will work.

Step 5b: Evaluate Options

♦ **Discuss each option generated in Step 4.**

Does it meet the criteria you think
are important?

♦ **Combine options or parts of options.**

Does the newly created option meet
the criteria?

Punishment and fault finding are not
options that solve problems.

Step 6: Create an Agreement

♦ Listen to understand the agreement.

♦ Show your support for the agreement or show you do not support the agreement.

♦ If you do not support the agreement, say why.

♦ Help the group make a plan to decide exactly how the solution will be carried out:

   "Who, what, when, where, and how?"

♦ Agree to do your part to make the solution work.

The Peaceable School
Group-Problem-Solving Process

STEP 1: AGREE TO PROBLEM SOLVE

♦ Listen for the purpose of the meeting.

♦ Follow the group-problem-solving rules:

> Participants sit in a circle.

> Every member of the class is responsible for communication *(listening and speaking)*. This means that each member is responsible for sharing his or her point of view about the problem if it has not already been shared by another.

> The *"Rule of Focus"* applies to all discussion. This means that whoever is speaking will be allowed to talk without being interrupted.

> Participants show respect for others. This means no criticism or sarcasm toward group members or their ideas.

> Each time someone in the group finishes making a statement, another group member summarizes and clarifies it before anyone else goes on to a new idea.

♦ Listen for and think about any special rules for this particular meeting.

STEP 2: GATHER POINTS OF VIEW

♦ Participate in the discussion *(listen and speak)*.

♦ Tell what you know and how you feel about the problem:

> Speak to be understood.

> Do not place blame.

> Speak if your point of view has not already been stated by another group member.

♦ Help the group decide on the problem statement. The problem statement tells exactly what problem you are trying to solve.

STEP 3: FOCUS ON INTERESTS IN THE GROUP

♦ Tell what you want in the situation and why you want what you want.

♦ If you don't know what you want and why:

> Tell why you think the problem is not going away.

> Tell what you think is likely to happen if the group cannot agree on a solution.

STEP 4: CREATE WIN-WIN OPTIONS

♦ Suggest ideas that will address the interests of group members.

♦ Follow the brainstorming rules:

Say any idea that comes to mind.

Do not judge or discuss ideas.

Come up with as many ideas as possible.

Try to think of unusual ideas.

STEP 5A: ESTABLISH CRITERIA TO EVALUATE OPTIONS

♦ Decide what criteria are important to consider. For example:

Does the option follow our school's rights and responsibilities?

Does the option help everyone involved?

Is the option fair?

Can the option solve the problem?

Can the group do it?

STEP 5B: EVALUATE OPTIONS

♦ Discuss each option generated in Step 4.

Does it meet the criteria you think are important?

♦ Combine options or parts of options.

Does the newly created option meet the criteria?

STEP 6: CREATE AN AGREEMENT

♦ Listen to understand the agreement.

♦ Show your support for the agreement or show you do not support the agreement.

♦ If you do not support the agreement, say why.

♦ Help the group make a plan to decide exactly how the solution will be carried out: *"Who, what, when, where, and how?"*

♦ Agree to do your part to make the solution work.